In Search of
POMPEII

In Search of
POMPEII

Uncovering a buried Roman city

Written and illustrated by
Giovanni Caselli

For Sara

Editor: Penny Clarke

Published in the United States in 1999
by Peter Bedrick Books
A division of NTC/Contemporary
Publishing Group, Inc.
4255 West Touhy Avenue
Lincolnwood (Chicago), Illinois 60646-1975
U.S.A.

Acknowledgments

The author and publishers would like to thank Judith
Lange, Rome, for use of the photographs on pages 36-37.

Library of Congress Cataloging-in-Publication Data

Caselli, Giovanni, 1939-
  In search of Pompeii: uncovering a buried Roman city / written
and illustrated by Giovanni Caselli.
    p. cm. -- (In search of)
  Includes index.
  Summary: Describes the discovery and excavation of the ruins of the ancient
city of Pompeii, buried by the eruption of Mount Vesuvius in 79 A.D., and
what has been learned about life there.
  ISBN 0-87226-545-5 (hc.)
  1. Pompeii (Extinct city)--Discovery and exploration Juvenile literature.
2. Time capsules--Italy Juvenile literature. 3. Pompeii (Extinct city)--Social life
and customs Juvenile literature. 4. Excavations (Archaeology) --Italy
--Pompeii--(Extinct city) Juvenile literature.
[1. Pompeii (Extinct city) 2. Excavations (Archaeology)--Italy--Pompeii (Extinct
city)]
1.Title. II. Title: Pompeii. III. Series.
DG70.P7C33 1999
937'.7--dc21   99-21352
                                                CIP

Printed in Hong Kong / China

International Standard Book Number:
0-87226-545-5

99 00 01 02 03 15 14 13 12 11 10 9 8 7 6 5 4 3 2 1

Contents

August 24, AD79

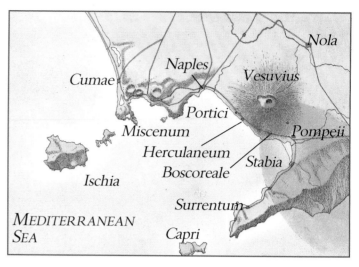

When the volcano Vesuvius erupted on August 24, AD79, it destroyed a rich and thickly populated part of southern Italy. We know that from the archaeological discoveries at Herculaneum and, especially, at Pompeii. But, more remarkably, we know what the disaster was actually like for the people who lived in the region. The young Roman nobleman Pliny the Younger witnessed the eruption and wrote a letter that is the earliest known account of such a tragedy.

The Bay of Naples, AD79

Vesuvius dominates the region—one of the most densely populated parts of Roman Italy. Ash falls from the eruption affected the area around Pompeii and Stabia, but lava covered Herculaneum.

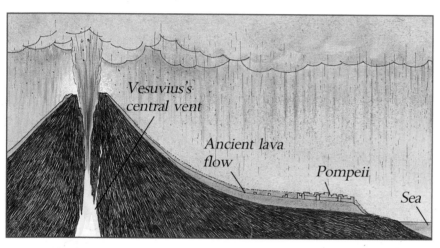

Unknown danger

Until it erupted in AD79, no one living in the region realized Vesuvius was a volcano. Now we know that Pompeii was built on an old lava flow and that the region's fertile soil is the result of eruptions in prehistoric times. Once Vesuvius began to erupt, the inhabitants in the towns around the Bay of Naples did not have a chance to escape unscathed.

Eyewitness

As people screamed and struggled to escape the horror, Pliny described the eruption as looking like "a pine tree, for it shot up to a great height in the form of a trunk, which extended itself at the top into several branches."

Unexpected terror

"Ashes now fall upon us, though as yet not in great quantity. I looked behind me; gross darkness pressed upon our rear, and came rolling over the land after us like a torrent . . . darkness overspread us, not like that of a moonless or cloudy night, but of a room when it is shut up, and the lamp put out. You could hear the shrieks of women, the crying of children, and the shouts of men; some were seeking their children, others their parents, others their wives or husbands . . . one lamenting his own fate, another that of his family . . . many lifting their hands to the gods; but the greater part imagining that there were no gods left and that the last and eternal night was come upon the world." This description from Pliny the Younger's letter to Tacitus is as vivid now as when he wrote it almost 2,000 years ago.

Too late

Pliny the Elder, keen to study the eruption at close range, waited too long to escape. The Roman scientist lost his life, together with thousands of other people in the area.

A survivor's letter

Pliny the Younger (right) was 17 when he saw the eruption. His letter describing it to his friend Tacitus is the only eyewitness account of the catastrophe. Part of the letter is reproduced above.

11

The buried cities

Pompeii remained buried and forgotten for about 1,670 years, although the plateau where it had once stood was always known as "Civita" (the City).

In 1592, Domenico Fontana, a distinguished architect, was hired to dig a tunnel across the Civita to take water from the River Sarno to the town of Torre Annunziata. As his workmen were cutting the tunnel they discovered the basements of buildings, inscriptions, statues and wall paintings, but the discoveries aroused no interest. In 1689 a stone with the inscription POMPEIA was discovered in the ruins. But this, too, was ignored and soon forgotten.

An inscription found in the late 17th century. This view of it is taken from an engraving by Piranesi.

Bay of Naples

In 1748, Don Rocco de Alcubierre, a Spanish engineer, heard rumors that workers had found the ruins of houses. He believed they might belong to the city buried in the eruption of AD79.

In April of that year, Alcubierre started digging (left) in the street today known as Via della Fortuna.

Doric temple

VIEW OVER THE SITE OF POMPEII, LATE 17TH CENTURY

Unexcavated area

Large theater

Odeon

Gladiators' barracks

Unexcavated area

Excavations had only just begun when workers discovered the ruins of the neighboring city of Herculaneum, diverting interest and attention from Pompeii. In 1754, when excavations at Pompeii began again, a "dig diary"—a proper record of discoveries—was kept for the first time.

Recording the discoveries

Among the earliest people who recorded finds at Pompeii was Domenico Fontana, shown above. Later visitors to Pompeii included the Italian architect and engraver Giovanni Piranesi (1720-78), who made many drawings of the site and its remains. Detailed and very accurate, his drawings are an important record of the work.

13

It's Pompeii!

For many years the ruins were believed to be those of the town of Stabia. Then, on November 27, 1756, the name Pompeii appears in the excavation diary for the first time, although no one now knows why the correct identification was made at last.

The excavations were somewhat haphazard, and work was slow. Most of it was done by convicts and slaves who worked chained in pairs. Even so, many spectacular discoveries were made late in the 18th century. The most important of these were the soldiers' quarters, the villa of Diomedes, the odeon and the theater.

Convict working at Pompeii

A scholarly visitor

The English scholar Sir William Gell (1777-1836) visited Pompeii many times to study the ruins. He illustrated his book, *Pompeiana*, with reconstructions of the ruined buildings.

Unexcavated area

Doric temple

Stunning

This mosaic (above), found at Pompeii, shows Alexander the Great's victory over the armies of Darius, King of Persia, at the battle of Gaugamela in 331BC.

VIEW OVER THE SITE OF POMPEII, 18TH TO EARLY 19TH CENTURY

Unexcavated area

Large theater

Odeon

Gladiators' barracks

Unexcavated area

Johann Joachim Winckelmann

This great German antiquarian visited the excavations at Herculaneum and Pompeii in 1762, and wrote enthusiastic letters about them to his friends.

Tourist trail

By the end of the 18th century many wealthy northern Europeans were making the "Grand Tour," visiting historic and beautiful places in the south. Pompeii was usually on their route.

The great enterprise

In December 1860, Victor Emmanuel II, king of the newly united Italy, appointed Giuseppe Fiorelli Director of the Excavations at Pompeii. The era of scientific excavation had begun.

Fiorelli divided the city into quarters or regions and, within each one, gave every block and building a number, a system which is still used today.

House of the Tragic Poet

Temple of Jupiter (Capitol)

Forum baths

Vesuvian gate

House of the Golden Cupids

House of Lucius Caecilius Jucundus

Forum

Central baths

Stabian baths

Unexcavat

Temple of Venus

Government buildings

Eumachia

Doric temple

A lifetime's work

Amedeo Maiuri (left) carried on the excavation work begun by Fiorelli. Director of archaeology from 1924 to 1961, Maiuri made many important discoveries.

Temple of Isis

Gladiators' barracks

Grand theater

Small theater

Stabian gate

House of the Citharist

International interest

Archaeologists from all over the world came to see Fiorelli's work at Pompeii.

Discovering the people of Pompeii

The eruption overwhelmed Pompeii so quickly that many of the people trying to flee were buried by the falling ash.

In the centuries that followed, the ash hardened and the bodies decayed until all that remained of Pompeii's people were human-shaped spaces where they had fallen.

As the archaeologists worked they discovered these spaces in the hardened ash. By filling them with plaster they revealed the forms of some of the people who lived in Pompeii in AD79.

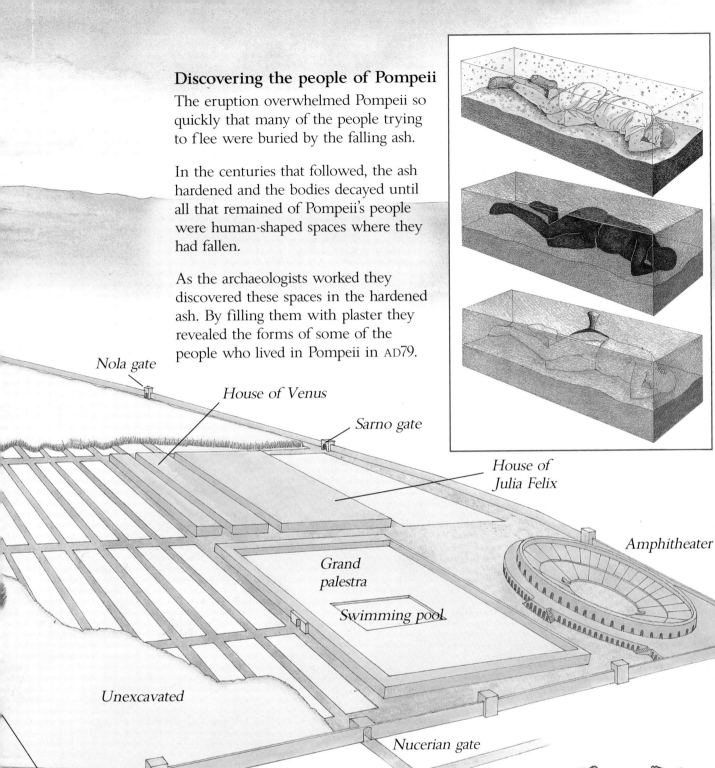

Nola gate

House of Venus

Sarno gate

House of Julia Felix

Amphitheater

Grand palestra

Swimming pool

Unexcavated

Nucerian gate

House of Menander

Painstaking work

Slowly and carefully soil and volcanic debris were removed. The position of every fragment of plaster and brickwork was recorded and then restored to its original place. Charred wood was replaced by a replica in fresh timber. It is thanks to the work of Maiuri that so much of Pompeii can be seen today.

Forced labor

Even in the 20th century convicts were used as laborers at the site.

17

Pompeii: August 23, AD79

The city sleeps under the scorching sun as most of its 20,000 inhabitants take a siesta, unaware of the forces building up within Vesuvius, less than six miles (ten kilometers) away. Small tremors shake the houses, a few flakes of plaster fall from the walls, but earthquakes are common and the city keeps going as usual. No one knows that the plateau on which the city is built is a lava flow from an ancient eruption and that very soon there will be another.

As the afternoon draws to a close and the temperature begins to cool, many of Pompeii's inhabitants will go to one of the three public baths. Men will saunter up to the oldest part of the city, where the forum and public buildings are, to meet friends, discuss politics and gossip in the shade of the colonnades around the forum.

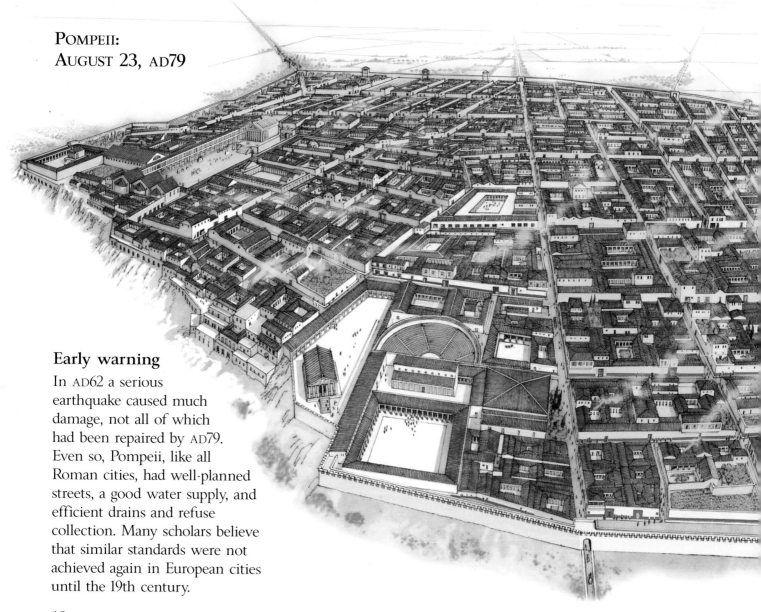

POMPEII:
AUGUST 23, AD79

Early warning

In AD62 a serious earthquake caused much damage, not all of which had been repaired by AD79. Even so, Pompeii, like all Roman cities, had well-planned streets, a good water supply, and efficient drains and refuse collection. Many scholars believe that similar standards were not achieved again in European cities until the 19th century.

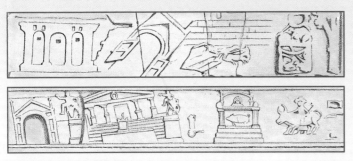

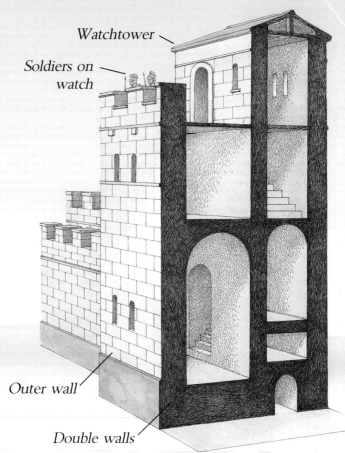

Watchtower

Soldiers on watch

Outer wall

Double walls

Reliefs from the house of Lucius Caecilius Jucundus vividly depict the earthquake of AD62.

The city's streets

The streets are paved with hard-wearing volcanic stone. Crosswalks of raised stones help pedestrians get from one sidewalk to another.

Pompeii's defenses

For much of its two-mile (three-kilometer) length, the city's wall follows the edge of the lava flow. Built of volcanic tufa, the wall has watchtowers and eight fortified gates.

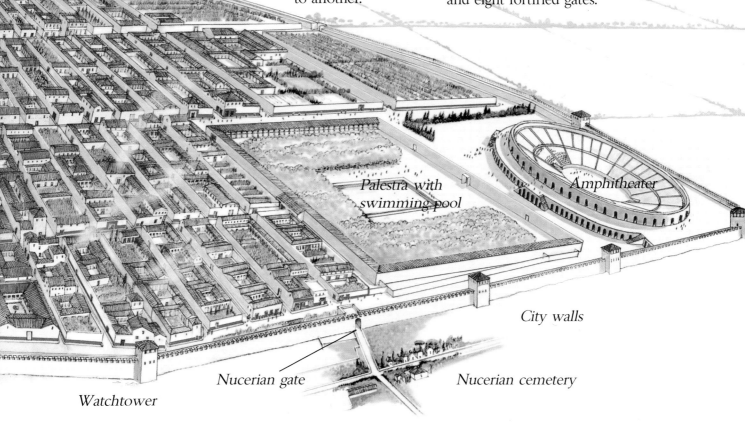

Palestra with swimming pool

Amphitheater

City walls

Nucerian gate

Nucerian cemetery

Watchtower

19

The forum

The forum was the heart of all Roman towns and cities. It was the center of administration, politics, religion and commerce, and ranged around it were all the city's most important buildings.

The forum at Pompeii is the best preserved of any Roman city. The great rectangle is surrounded by a colonnaded portico. Above this is a gallery or loggia, its roof supported on slim columns.

At one end is the Capitol, the Temple of Jupiter. West of the forum is the basilica, Pompeii's most imposing public building.

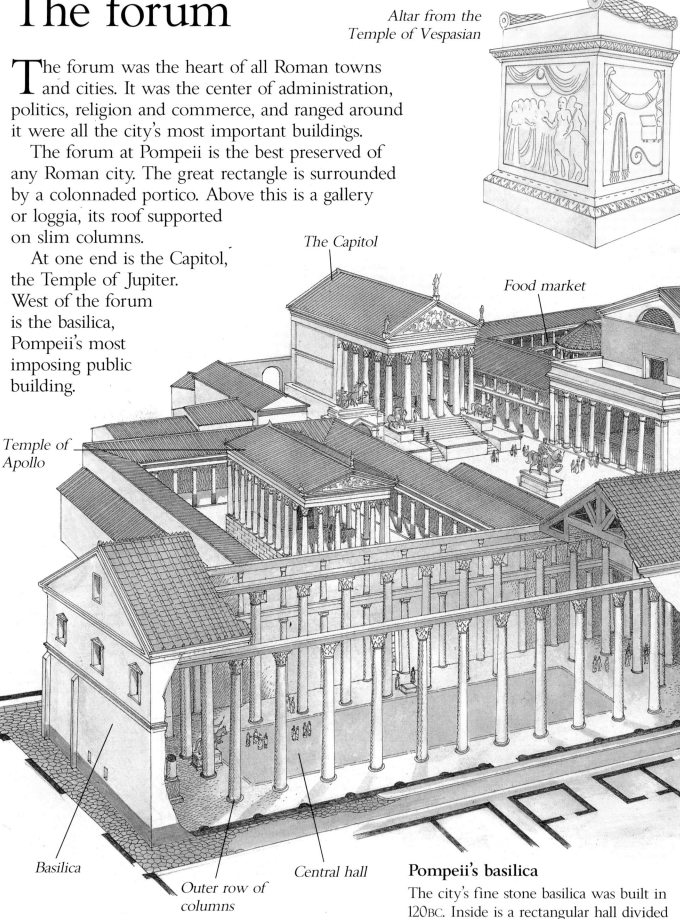

The Capitol

Food market

Temple of Apollo

Basilica

Outer row of columns

Central hall

Pompeii's basilica

The city's fine stone basilica was built in 120BC. Inside is a rectangular hall divided into three aisles by rows of columns.

Around the forum are several temples. The Temple of the Lares is dedicated to the city's protecting spirits. Next to it is the Temple of Vespasian. He had ruled the Roman Empire since AD69 and died a month before Vesuvius erupted. Beside the temple is the sanctuary of the priestess Eumachia. Over the years it became the city's stock exchange and a center of political power.

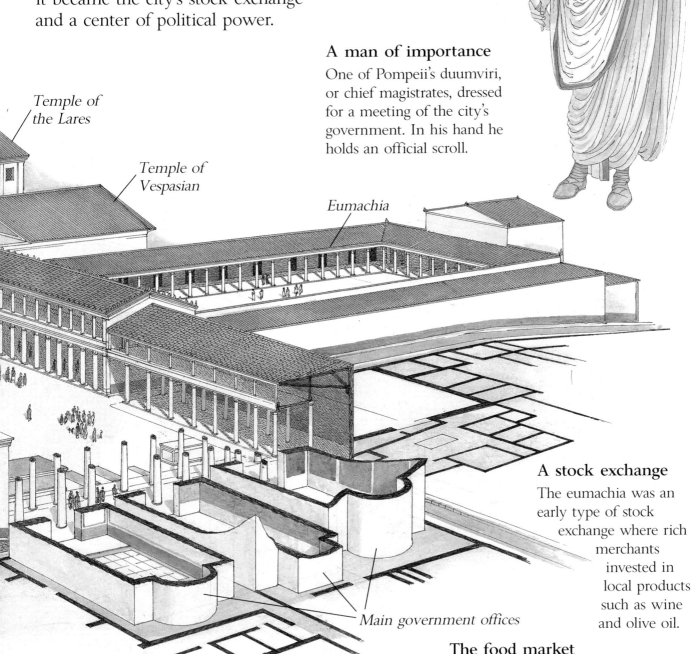

A man of importance

One of Pompeii's duumviri, or chief magistrates, dressed for a meeting of the city's government. In his hand he holds an official scroll.

Temple of the Lares

Temple of Vespasian

Eumachia

Main government offices

A stock exchange

The eumachia was an early type of stock exchange where rich merchants invested in local products such as wine and olive oil.

The food market

On the east of the forum, next to the Capitol, is the food market. The fish market is set apart in a large recessed bay. In addition to the shops and stalls in the market, shops are set into two of the outside walls.

Government offices

Pompeii's principal government offices, opposite the Capitol, open directly onto the forum.

The gods of Pompeii

The Romans believed they were surrounded by supernatural forces represented by gods and goddesses. They followed strict rules so as not to offend these beings who might otherwise become angry. Priests interpreted "signs," which could range from a pattern of clouds to the intestines of a sacrificed animal, to find out what actions the government or ordinary people should take. The Romans did not believe in an afterlife, or think they had a soul.

Head of Jupiter

Section through the Temple of Jupiter

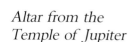

Altar from the Temple of Jupiter

The Temple of Apollo

Smaller than the Temple of Jupiter, this temple (below) does not open directly onto the forum. It is set in a square with a colonnade around it.

The Temple of Jupiter

The Temple of Jupiter in the forum (above and below) was also sacred to Juno and Minerva and was Pompeii's most important temple. Like most Roman temples, it is built on a podium, with a portico at the front, two colonnades inside and three cells, one for each deity. The temple was badly damaged by the earthquake in AD62 and was still in ruins when Vesuvius erupted 17 years later.

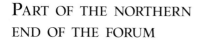

PART OF THE NORTHERN END OF THE FORUM

Temple of Apollo

Cross section through the colonnade around the forum

Triumphal arch

Temple of Jupiter

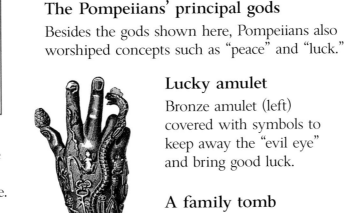

Jupiter *Juno* *Venus* *Mars*

The Pompeiians' principal gods

Besides the gods shown here, Pompeiians also worshiped concepts such as "peace" and "luck."

Household gods

Each home had a shrine to the Lares, the spirits who protected the home. Not all shrines were as grand as this; many were just a niche in the wall.

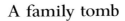

Lucky amulet

Bronze amulet (left) covered with symbols to keep away the "evil eye" and bring good luck.

A family tomb

This cross section through a family tomb (right) shows the funerary urns in position.

Priestess of Isis

Isis was a goddess first worshiped by the Egyptians.

Roman cemeteries

Roman cemeteries (below) were always outside the walls of a town or city. The most important cemetery at Pompeii was just beyond the Herculaneum gate. The tombs flanked the main road.

Cremation

The Romans did not bury their dead—instead they cremated them. They put the ashes in a small urn which was placed in a much larger funerary urn. This was put in the family's tomb.

Herculaneum gate *Tombs* *Family tomb*

Entertainment

Every Roman city and town of any size had at least an amphitheater and a theater. Pompeii was no exception. It had a large open-air theater for drama performances, a covered theater (or "odeon") for music and poetry, and an amphitheater seating 20,000 spectators for games and gladiator fights. On the outskirts there would also have been a hippodrome, a track for chariot races.

Pompeii's theater

The large theater, built into a natural hollow in the plateau on which Pompeii stands, could seat 5,000 people.

Brutal entertainments

The amphitheater, built in 80BC, is the oldest one known. Rome's amphitheater, the Colosseum, was not built until AD96. Fights between gladiators were held in the amphitheater during religious or civic festivals. Men from the nearby mountains made the best gladiators, because they fought hardest. The killing of wild animals let loose in the arena was becoming popular at the time Vesuvius erupted.

Small bronze statue of a gladiator from Pompeii

The end of the fight

As a slave blows a ceremonial trumpet, a man dressed as a demon kills the injured gladiators with a blow of his hammer.

Ceremonial trumpeter

"Demon" with sledgehammer

Dragging a body away

Victors and vanquished

Performances on stage

Pompeii's theater was built between 200 and 150BC. It was later enlarged, and by AD79 could seat an audience of 5,000. Acting was fairly stylized, and actors wore masks to show the type of role they were playing. Women were not allowed to act. Actors playing cymbals and a tambourine (below) were a feature of Pompeiian entertainment, just as they are in today's traditional Neapolitan theater.

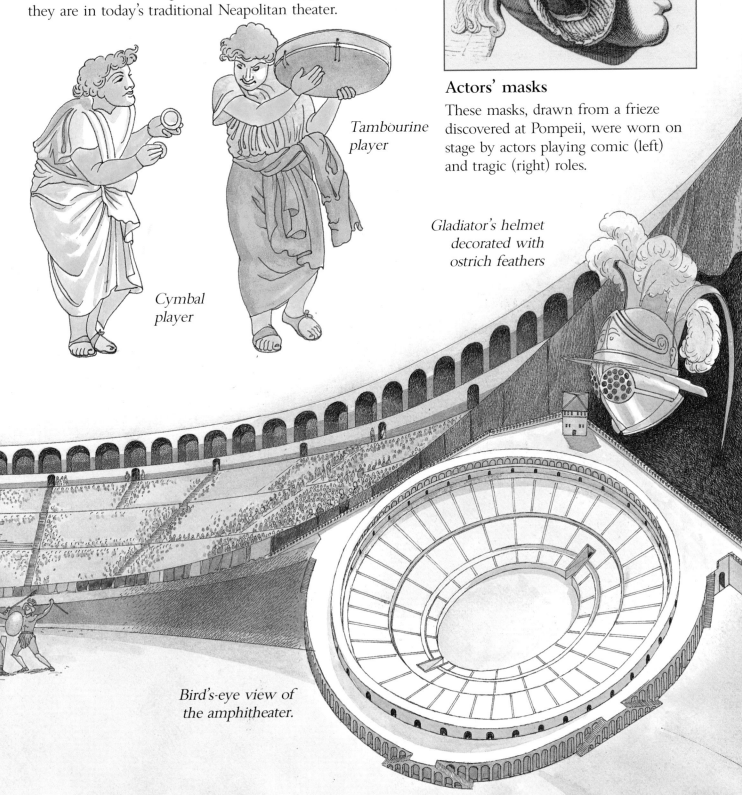

Tambourine player

Cymbal player

Actors' masks

These masks, drawn from a frieze discovered at Pompeii, were worn on stage by actors playing comic (left) and tragic (right) roles.

Gladiator's helmet decorated with ostrich feathers

Bird's-eye view of the amphitheater.

The public baths

Pompeii had at least three public baths: the Stabian baths, the forum baths and the central baths, each in a different part of the city. The Stabian baths are the oldest, dating from the 2nd century BC. Like all Roman baths, those in Pompeii were not just places to wash. They were social centers, where men and women met to exchange gossip or discuss more serious matters.

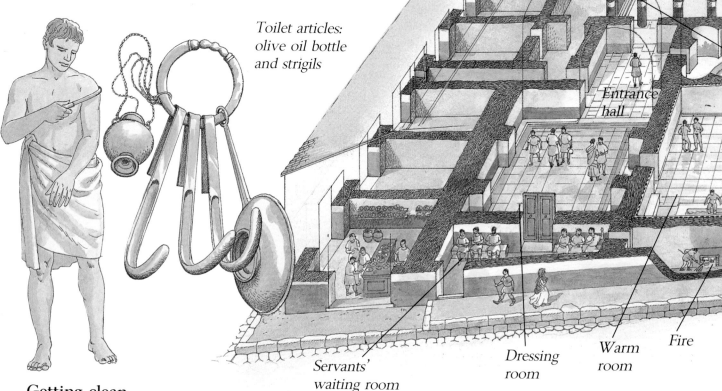

Toilet articles: olive oil bottle and strigils

Cold bath

Row of shops

Entrance hall

Servants' waiting room

Dressing room

Warm room

Fire

Getting clean

Romans did not have soap. They put olive oil on their skin, then scraped off dirt and oil with a strigil (scraper).

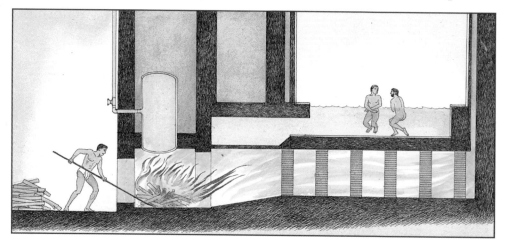

Heating the baths

The baths were centrally heated. Underground, slaves kept fires blazing beneath boilers to heat the water. The hot air from the fires also heated the building. The baths were built so that the hot air passed under the floors of the baths, which were supported on brick columns, and up behind the walls of the pools. The hot bath or "calidarium" was nearest the furnaces, the cold bath or "frigidarium" the furthest.

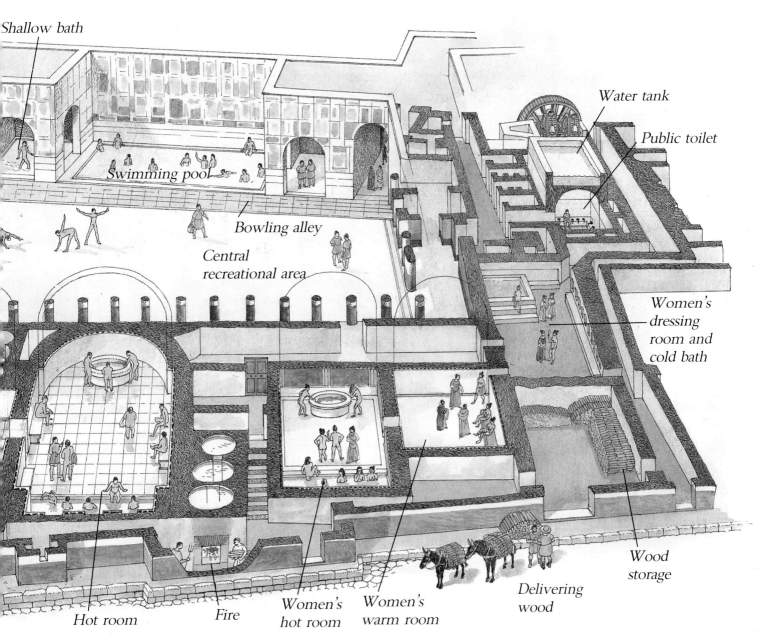

Shallow bath

Swimming pool

Bowling alley

Central
recreational area

Water tank

Public toilet

Women's
dressing
room and
cold bath

Hot room

Fire

Women's
hot room

Women's
warm room

Delivering
wood

Wood
storage

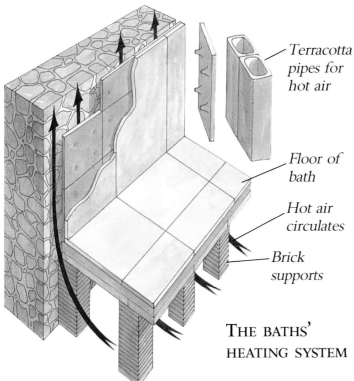

Terracotta
pipes for
hot air

Floor of
bath

Hot air
circulates

Brick
supports

THE BATHS'
HEATING SYSTEM

Public toilets

The public baths, like all public buildings,
had efficient and hygienic public toilets
where people sat, chatting or discussing
more important topics. Romans used
sponges on sticks to wipe their bottoms.

Sponge
on stick

27

Ordinary lives

Most Pompeiians were craftsmen or traders providing food, clothes, household goods and services for themselves and their masters. Much of the hard manual work was done by slaves—even fairly poor people would have a slave or two. Although some fine houses belonging to wealthy Pompeiians survived the eruption, most people lived in small apartments above or at the back of shops, and few of these have survived. Slaves slept in their masters' houses or where they worked.

A Pompeiian take-out

Most Pompeiians had no cooking facilities in their cramped little homes, so they bought cooked food from "fast-food" shops. One has survived so well that it has been possible to reconstruct it (above). At the back of the shop was a room where customers could eat and drink in private. A 19th-century engraving (left) of a wall painting found at Pompeii suggests what such a room might have been like.

Part of Forum Street

The Temple of Fortuna (Good Luck) (left) stood on Forum Street. Between the shops are staircases leading to second-floor apartments.

VIEW OF FORUM STREET

Temple of Fortuna

Homes above shops

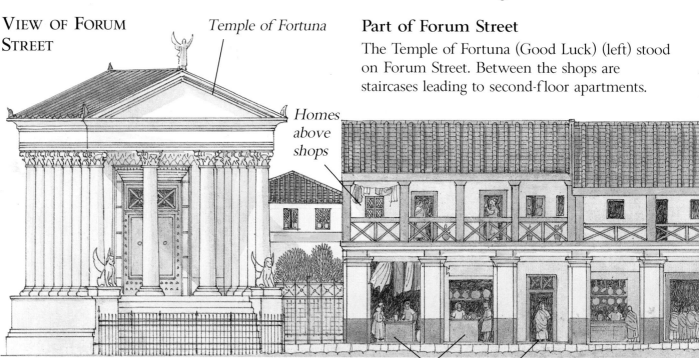

Shops

Entrance to stairs to upper floor

Baking bread

A slave puts a loaf in the oven to bake. Bread was baked in ovens like this in many parts of Europe until well into the 20th century.

Ancient loaves

Loaves of bread drawn as they were found at Pompeii in the 19th century.

Grinding grain for flour

The remains of one bakery were so complete that it was easy to reconstruct. The baker did everything on site, from grinding the flour to selling the finished loaves. The flour mill (left) was made of two volcanic stones. As grain was fed into a hole in the top, slaves turned it, grinding the grain against the lower, cone-shaped stone. The flour came out at the base. Sometimes donkeys turned the mill instead of slaves.

The flour mill

This cross section of the flour mill shows the shape of the two stones, where the grain is fed in at the top, and also the wooden apparatus for turning the mill.

Roofs tiled with terracotta tiles

Doorway to stairs to upper floor

Open-fronted shop

Stairs to upper floor

29

Lives of the rich

Roman society was ruthlessly capitalist. Two inscriptions from houses in Pompeii sum it up: "Lucrum gaudium" (My earnings are my joy), scribbled on a wall, and "Salve lucru" (Hello profit) from the house of two businessmen.

There was no public aid for the sick or unemployed. If a merchant went bankrupt he lost everything. Nevertheless the Roman Empire was rich and its people prosperous—as the homes of the wealthy in Pompeii show. The houses were centered around a large, open hall or "atrium," with other rooms opening off it. Outside was a large courtyard or garden with a colonnaded peristyle around it.

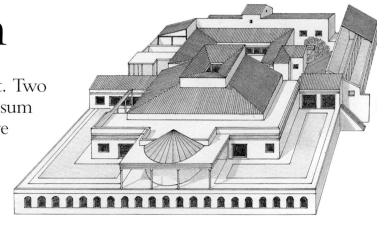

The Villa of Mysteries

The grandest of all Pompeii's villas is the Villa of Mysteries ("Villa dei Misteri" in Italian). This vast, 90-room mansion was built in the 3rd century BC, and is outside the city, a little way along the road to Herculaneum. It was excavated and restored from 1909 to 1930. It gets its name from its magnificent wall paintings, which show a mysterious ritual connected with Semele and the god Dionysus.

The House of the Tragic Poet

The house gets its name from the mosaics and wall paintings with which it is decorated, for all are inspired by the tragic poetry the Romans enjoyed. Although it is a very beautiful house, it is by no means the grandest in Pompeii. It was built not many years before the eruption of Vesuvius.

Beware of the dog

Still on guard: the inscription on this mosaic found on the floor of the main entrance of the House of the Tragic Poet reads "Cave canem" (Beware of the dog).

CROSS SECTION OF THE
HOUSE OF THE TRAGIC POET

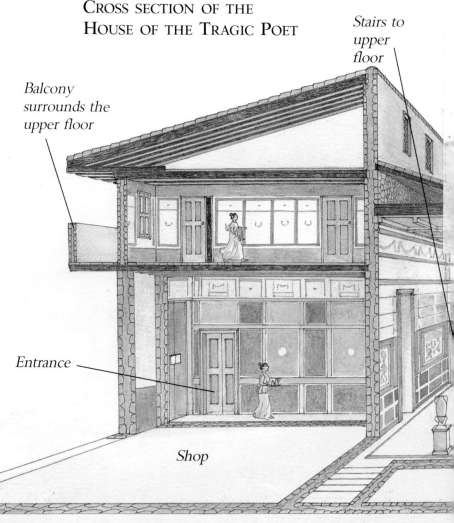

Stairs to upper floor

Balcony surrounds the upper floor

Entrance

Shop

The roofs of buildings

Buildings had roofs of terracotta tiles (right). This method of roofing, which had reached Italy from what is now Turkey in the 9th century BC, is still used in Tuscany.

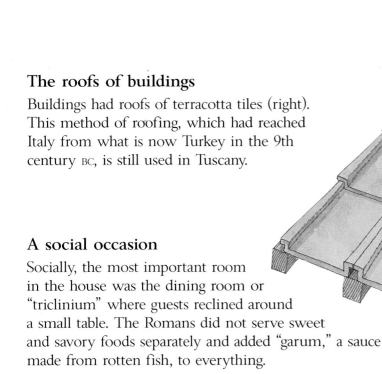

A social occasion

Socially, the most important room in the house was the dining room or "triclinium" where guests reclined around a small table. The Romans did not serve sweet and savory foods separately and added "garum," a sauce made from rotten fish, to everything.

Placement of guests around a dining table

A desire for privacy

Pompeii was a crowded, cramped city, but the rich made sure they enjoyed privacy by building high walls around their homes and gardens.

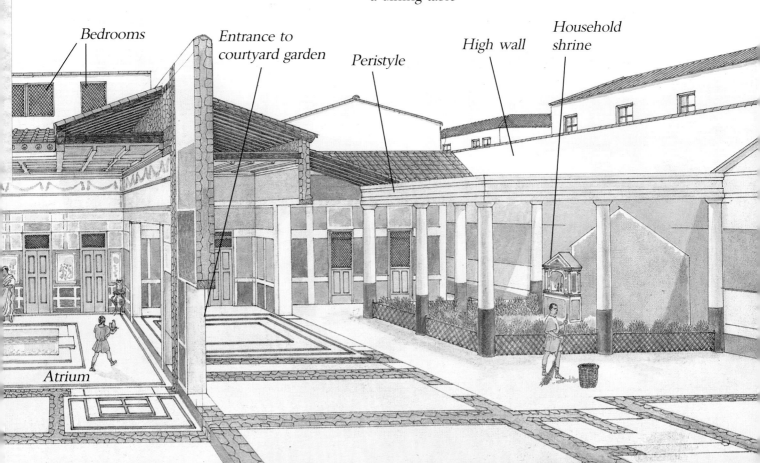

Bedrooms

Entrance to courtyard garden

Peristyle

High wall

Household shrine

Atrium

An unequal society

Roman, and therefore Pompeiian, society was entirely dominated by men. Men had absolute power over every member of their household, from their wives to their slaves. Legally, women had very few rights and a man could divorce his wife without giving any reason. When a baby was born it was laid at its father's feet and he decided whether it lived or was killed. Even if he let it live, the father had the right to sell it as a slave whenever he wanted to. Any man who could afford to kept at least two slaves as domestic servants. Slaves had some legal rights, but their master's interests came first.

Sabina Poppaea, wife of a wealthy Pompeiian

A magnificent home

A wealthy Pompeiian family in the atrium of their house. Men such as this owned hundreds of slaves.

Mirror

Gold earring

Like every Roman city, Pompeii's local council was based on the government of Rome. The two chief magistrates, or "duumviri," ran the government. They were assisted by two "aediles," who ran Pompeii on a day-to-day basis. The duumviri and the aediles were elected each year by all adult men who were not slaves or foreigners. The posts were unpaid and the holders had to pay everyone they employed, so only the very rich could afford to hold these positions.

Between 80 and 100 "optimates" (wealthy and honorable citizens) made up the city council. They held office for life and acted as advisers to the government. They met in the curia, the city's municipal room.

Toga

Color of strip shows status

A man of power

One of Pompeii's two duumviri, dressed for a military parade through the city.

Female slaves

Pretty female slaves fetched high prices at the slave market but, like all slaves, they had few rights. They helped in the house, served at dinner parties and looked after children.

TENEMENE
FVGIA·ET·REVO
CAMEADDOMNVM
EVVIVENTIVM·IN
ARACALLISTI

A sign of ownership

Many slaves had to wear a disc giving the name of their owner in case they ran away. The inscription on the disc above gives the name of the slave's owner and asks the person who finds the slave to take him back. The slave on the left probably had to wear a similar disc.

Electioneering

Elections were frequent and though the Romans had no newspapers (printing had not been invented) the walls of buildings were good places to write election slogans. Amazingly, many have survived, and a selection is shown below.

Pompeii and its people

Pompeii had about 20,000 inhabitants, of whom 8,000 were slaves. It was a rigidly divided society, with everyone knowing—and apparently accepting—their place. Because of the speed with which the eruption of Vesuvius overwhelmed the city, we know more about the lives of these people who lived almost 2,000 years ago than about many more recent societies.

A woman's life

Pompeiian women were supposed to be decorative, not clever, although a few read and wrote poetry.

Successful businessman

Lucius Caecilius Jucundus was a rich moneylender: 150 tablets recording his business dealings were found during excavations of his home.

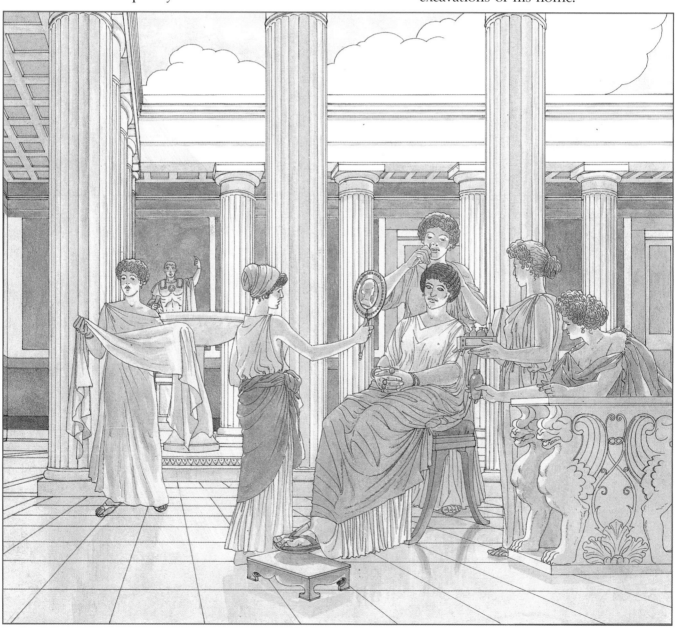

Signs of the times

Signs like these were common outside Pompeii's shops. Each shop and trade had its own distinctive pictures and symbols.

Sign for a grocer: two men carrying a wine amphora

Butchers' signs showed animals

The wrong side of town

This reconstruction of a grocer's shop, with homes for poorer Pompeiians above it, is in sharp contrast with the reconstruction of the home of a rich family (opposite). Instead of the cool, enclosed atrium, the shop and balconies outside the apartments above are open to the noise of the street all year round. In winter there is little shelter from the rain, and in summer none from heat and dust. The contents of slop buckets emptied from the balconies splatters the goods for sale below.

Lighting homes

At night, homes were quite dark. The wealthy had metal lamps (above), but most people used little terracotta ones. Neither kind gave much light.

Pompeii: the evidence

Much of our knowledge of Roman life comes from the evidence uncovered at Pompeii. Splendid houses, beautiful paintings, sculptures of bronze and marble, fine glass, metal, and pottery bear witness not only to a city that perished in one day but to a long-vanished civilization.

A visit to Pompeii is like entering a time machine: you can see wide streets still with the ruts cut in the paving stones by the wheels of chariots, the entrance to a shop with graffiti on the wall beside it, the baths and grand houses with their wall paintings and colonnaded gardens. But, above all, there are the people of Pompeii, overwhelmed as they tried to escape the horror that overtook their city. Across nearly 2,000 years, their twisted bodies are vivid witnesses of what happened on August 24, AD79.

A grand house

In the center of the most exclusive Pompeiian houses was a garden area surrounded by a colonnade (a covered walkway with columns).

Pompeiian streets

The grand public thoroughfare (top) leads to the forum. On the left is the Capitol. A smaller street (above) contains houses and shops in a remarkable state of preservation. The sidewalks and crosswalk of raised stones are as usable today as they were nearly 2,000 years ago.

Fancy living room

The main reception room of this house is decorated with painted columns, which echo the real ones in the garden area beyond. Painted on the wall in between the columns are scenes of rural life.

A cold plunge

One end of the frigidarium (cold pool) in the forum baths. Meeting friends here would have been a welcome relief from the heat of the Pompeiian summer.

Status symbols

Decorated columns and a frieze in the tepidarium (warm pool) of the forum baths. The richness of the decoration is a good indication of the wealth of the city.

Timely warning

The craftsman who made the above mosaic at the entrance to a house left no doubt that the watchdog was fierce!

Stunning art

A wall painting (below) shows the head of Medusa, the mythical monster with snakes instead of hair.

An astonishing record

Pompeiians lie as they died (below) under the ash of Vesuvius's eruption. The actual bodies disintegrated long ago. What visitors see today are the casts that emerged when archaeologists filled with plaster the body-shaped cavities they uncovered in the hardened volcanic ash.

Chronology

Stone inscribed with Pompeii's name

BC

c 1000 The Etruscans from Asia Minor (Turkey) settle in Tuscany and the region of Naples.

c 753 Rome is founded on an Etruscan settlement on the River Tiber.

Priestess of Isis

c 550 First evidence of a settlement at Pompeii.

510 Rome begins the invasion of the rest of Italy.

474 The Greeks rule the area around Pompeii.

290 Rome's conquest of central Italy is complete.

89 All people in Italy conquered by the Romans are officially declared Roman citizens. Sulla, a Roman general, occupies Pompeii.

80 Sulla establishes Pompeii as a Roman colony.

AD

59 During gladiator games in Pompeii riots and running battles break out between citizens of Pompeii and those from the nearby town of Nuceria.

62 An earthquake destroys many buildings in Pompeii.

August 24, 79 Vesuvius erupts and destroys everything in the region.

View across Pompeii's harbor as Vesuvius erupts

*Altar from the
Temple of Vespasian*

104 Pliny the Younger writes accounts of the destruction of Pompeii for his friend, the historian Tacitus, so he can record it accurately in his *History of Rome*.

1592 Domenico Fontana, an architect from Rome, finds the ruins of Pompeii while digging a tunnel for a water supply.

1689 A stone with the inscription "Pompeii" is found among the ruins of the city, but nobody associates the name with the site.

1748 Don Rocco de Alcubierre is given permission to excavate at Pompeii.

1762 Johann Joachim Winckelmann, the German antiquarian, visits Pompeii.

*Amedeo Maiuri,
chief archaeologist
at Pompeii
1924-61*

1763 A tomb with the name "Pompeii" on it firmly establishes the city's identity.

*One of
Pompeii's
duumviri*

1860 Italy is united into one kingdom, and systematic excavations begin, directed by the archaeologist Giuseppe Fiorelli.

1924 The archaeologist Amedeo Maiuri takes over the excavations at Pompeii, working there until 1961. Much of what we know about Pompeii today is the result of his work.

*Mosaic of a
watchdog found in
the House of the
Tragic Poet*

39

Glossary

aedile One of the two junior magistrates who were responsible for the daily running of Roman towns and cities.

amphitheater Arena for gladiatorial games and other public entertainments.

amphora Large pottery storage jar, used for water, olive oil, garum or wine.

antiquarian A 19th-century word for archaeologist.

archaeologist Someone who studies human history and prehistory by excavating and studying their remains.

atrium The central hall of a Roman house. It was open in the center so rainwater could drain from the roof into a pool and then into a storage cistern. All the rooms of the house opened from the atrium.

basilica Large public building near the forum, where merchants and businessmen met; also used as a court of justice. It was usually the finest building in a Roman town or city.

Paving in Pompeii's streets

calidarium Hot room in a public bath.

citizen Roman who had the right to vote.

curia Meeting place of a town or city council.

duumvir One of the two senior magistrates who ran a Roman town or city.

forum Originally a marketplace, it became a large open area in a city, a place for holding public meetings and transacting business. All the principal public buildings and government offices of a town or city were ranged around it.

Cross section through Vesuvius as it erupts

frigidarium Cold room in a public bath.

garum Oily sauce used by the Romans at every meal. It was made by leaving barrels of fish to rot in the sun for several days. Garum was one of the main commodities of Roman trade, second only to wine.

gladiator Men trained to fight against each other or wild animals to provide entertainment for the public. Gladiators were usually slaves or prisoners.

Recording finds made at Pompeii in the 18th century

mosaic Wall or floor decoration made by setting small colored stone or glass squares into wet plaster.

palestra Gymnasium where athletes trained and exercised.

peristyle Colonnade around the garden or central courtyard in a Roman house.

strigil Metal scraper used to scrape dirt, oil and sweat off the skin.

tepidarium Warm room in a public bath.

Masks worn by actors in the theater at Pompeii

lava The molten rock ejected by a volcano.

magistrate A holder of high political office in Roman government. Magistrates helped to collect taxes and ensure that law and order were maintained. They were the most important officials in a city.

One of Pompeii's duumviri

Who's who in Pompeii

Alcubierre, Don Rocco de: Spanish soldier and engineer employed by the King of Spain in 1748 to excavate Pompeii and Herculaneum.

Fiorelli, Giuseppe (1807-82): The archaeologist responsible for excavations at Pompeii from 1860 until his death. He inaugurated scientific excavation and restoration at Pompeii.

Fontana, Domenico: Eminent 16th-century architect and engineer, whose laborers discovered the remains of Pompeii while cutting a tunnel for a water supply. The importance of the discovery was not recognized.

Gell, Sir William (1777-1836): English scholar whose book, *Pompeiana*, had beautiful illustrations of the ruins and their reconstructions.

Sir William Gell

Maiuri, Amedeo: Archaeologist who worked at Pompeii from 1924 to 1961. It is due to his work that we know so much about the city.

Johann Joachim Winckelmann

Pliny the Elder (Gaius Plinius Secundus) (23-79): A Roman magistrate, author and scholar. He was stationed at Miscenum under the Emperor Vespasian as admiral of the Roman fleet. He died in the eruption, which he wanted to observe from close quarters.

Pliny the Younger (Gaius Plinius Caecilius Secundus) (62-114): The nephew of Pliny the Elder and also an author and scholar. He was a friend of the Emperor Trajan and the historian Tacitus. The two letters he wrote to Tacitus are the source of almost all our knowledge about the actual eruption of Vesuvius in AD79.

Vespasian: Emperor of Rome AD70 to 79, he died a month before the eruption of Vesuvius.

Winckelmann, Johann Joachim (1717-68): German scholar and author of a *History of Art of the Ancients*. He visited the ruins of Herculaneum and Pompeii, and wrote enthusiastic descriptions of them in letters to his friends, thereby making the sites widely known.

Index

Excavations at Pompeii in the 18th century

The battle between Alexander the Great and King Darius of Persia

Tourists visiting Pompeii's ruins in the 18th century